W9-AJN-861

To Robert Barnshaw,
who taught me to love history
—SBQ

For Darnell Lloyd III
—RGC

Balzer + Bray is an imprint of HarperCollins Publishers.

The United States v. Jackie Robinson
Text copyright © 2018 by Sudipta Bardhan-Quallen
Illustrations copyright © 2018 by R. Gregory Christie
All rights reserved. Manufactured in China.
No part of this book may be used or reproduced in any manner whatsoever
without written permission except in the case of brief quotations embodied in critical
articles and reviews. For information address HarperCollins Children's Books,
a division of HarperCollins Publishers, 195 Broadway, New York, NY 10007.
www.harpercollinschildrens.com
ISBN 978-0-06-228784-7 (trade bdg.)

The artist used acryla gouache to create the illustrations for this book.
Typography by Rachel Zegar
19 20 21   SCP   10 9 8 7 6 5 4 3 2
❖
First Edition

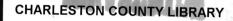

THE UNITED STATES
V.
Jackie Robinson

Written by **Sudipta Bardhan-Quallen**

Illustrated by R. Gregory Christie

BALZER + BRAY
An Imprint of HarperCollins*Publishers*

Long before anyone had heard of Rosa Parks, a guy named Jack refused to move to the back of the bus. And like Rosa, Jack made history, too.

Jack Robinson grew up in Pasadena, California, at a time when the public pools were open to black children only once a week—then drained immediately afterward and refilled with fresh water for the white children who swam the rest of the time.

Segregation was the reality of American life. Most white people would not share schools, restaurants, bathrooms, water fountains, or seating areas with black people. White lawmakers in the South actually passed laws requiring black people to stay away from places that were labeled "whites only."

As the only black family on their street, the Robinsons were not welcomed by their white neighbors. Some even started a petition to get the Robinsons to leave. But Jack's mother, Mallie, wouldn't go. She made it clear to any and all that she was not afraid and that she wouldn't allow anyone to treat her family badly.

Mallie taught her children to stand up for what was right, even when that was difficult to do.

Jack learned those lessons well.

Even as a child, Jack was good at sports—so much so that kids at school would bribe him with treats from their lunches if he played for *their* team. As he grew up, his name and athletic feats were regularly in the newspaper.

Jack and Mallie dreamed that his talent would unlock doors for him—especially to college. When the University of California, Los Angeles (UCLA) recruited Jack to play for them, that dream came true.

Jack became one of the most successful college athletes in the country. He won games, he broke records, he sealed championships.

But a lot of people still saw him only as a black man.

On the football field, opponents would go out of their way to hit him, whether he had the ball or not. Even Jack's own teammates once used practice as an excuse to tackle him so hard that they severely sprained his knee.

Black athletes weren't supposed to argue with white coaches, referees, or players. They were supposed to feel lucky that UCLA let them play at all. But Jack never forgot his mother's lessons. On or off the field, Jack wouldn't back down from anyone who treated him unfairly.

Jack became the first person in UCLA history to earn varsity letters in four different sports: football, basketball, baseball, and track. But that didn't mean he could start dreaming about a career in sports after college. There was a line that had to be crossed to play on a professional team—the color line. White athletes could be professionals, but no major team would hire a black player.

Jack couldn't bear to pursue a dream that would never come true. So he left college without graduating and looked to get a job.

Not long after, Pearl Harbor was attacked and the United States entered World War II. Americans from all walks of life—including Jack Robinson—answered their nation's call to defend freedom around the globe.

In the army, Jack experienced segregation on a daily basis. On the base there were separate places for black soldiers to sit and segregated barracks for them to live in. But for a long time, sports had been a place where Jack had been able to excel, regardless of the color of his skin. So one day, he tried to join the Fort Riley baseball team.

When Jack arrived at the field, players were already practicing. Jack introduced himself to the white officer in charge as a potential recruit.

The officer looked Jack over. He shook his head. Then he said, "You have to play for the colored team."

Except there was no colored team.

Jack hadn't realized army sports would have a color line too, or that the Fort Riley team wouldn't see him as just another baseball player.

But they only saw a black man.

Jack watched practice for a while, his face flushed with anger. Then he turned and walked away. But he didn't forget.

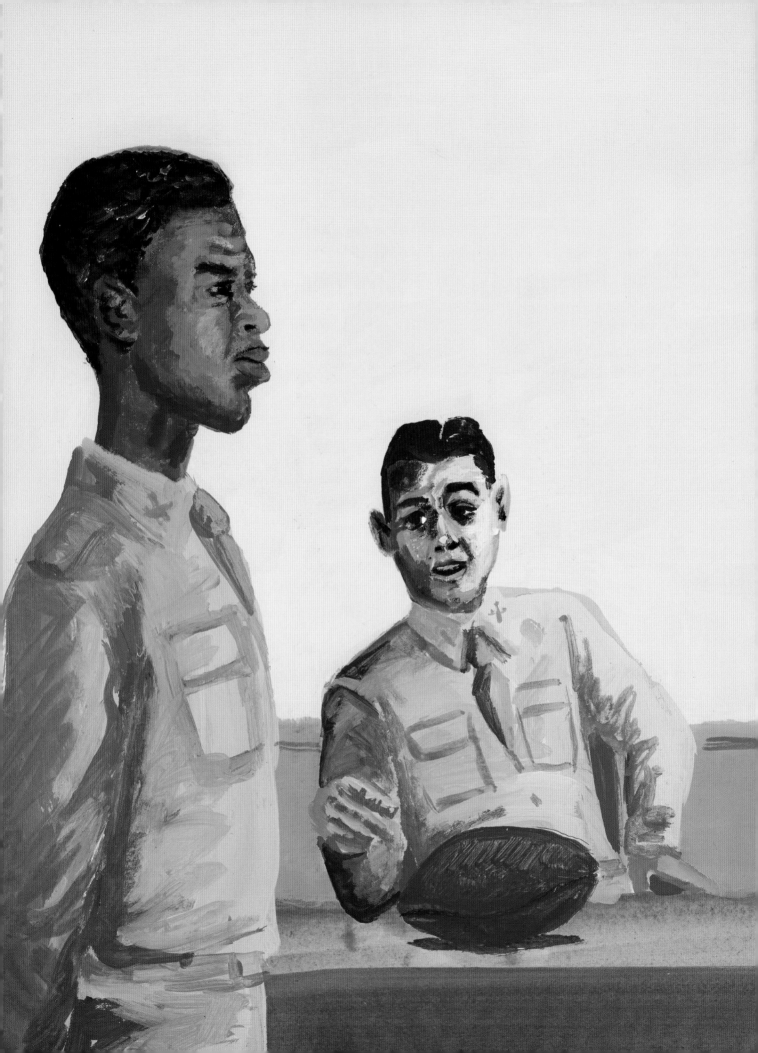

Soon afterward, a colonel asked Jack to play football for the base. Jack refused. The colonel sternly reminded Jack that he could be commanded to play.

Yes, Jack replied, but he couldn't be commanded to play *well*. "You wouldn't want me playing on your team," he said, "knowing my heart wasn't in it."

Jack never took a pitch or a snap for the army.

In May 1944, the army issued an order forbidding segregation on military posts and buses. To black soldiers like Jack, this was an important change. Even though segregation was found everywhere in America, from then on it was supposed to be different in the army. When Jack was on army property, he should've been free to go where he wanted.

But just because the army gave an order didn't mean that everyone respected it. Jack would soon learn that firsthand.

On July 6, at Fort Hood in Texas, Jack sat down in a seat in the middle of an army bus. He didn't notice other passengers staring at him or the driver telling him to go to the back.

The longer Jack ignored the driver, the more the man fumed. He stopped the bus and walked down the aisle. He balled his fist and said, "Will you move to the back?"

Jack knew his rights. He didn't argue. But he didn't get up, either. The driver glared. He warned Jack that there was trouble coming.

Within moments of the bus arriving at Jack's stop, a crowd of angry white people surrounded Jack, yelling at him to know his place, calling him names.

The crowd didn't see an officer in the United States Army. They only saw a black man.

When the military police arrived, they didn't detain any of the white people who had been shouting and making threats. They didn't discipline the bus driver for trying to segregate an army bus after the army had forbidden it. Instead, they decided that Jack Robinson was the one who was wrong.

Jack couldn't believe it. He'd been charged with two crimes. This wasn't a misunderstanding or a mistake. Jack would be taken to trial before a military court, called a court-martial. If he was found guilty, his army career would be over. He could go to jail.

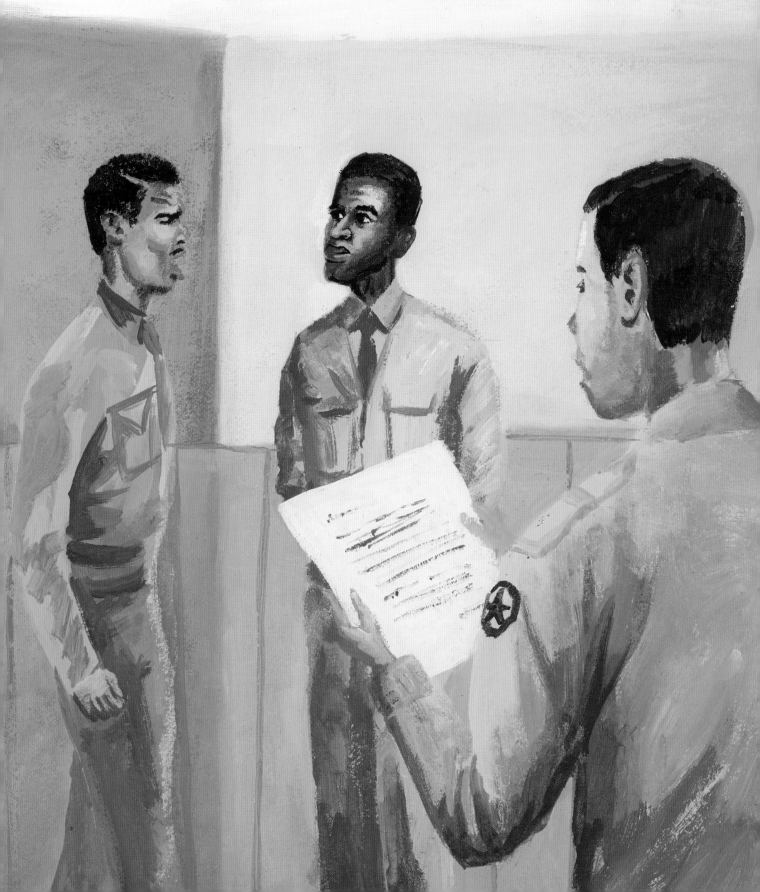

Jack knew the court-martial wouldn't have happened if he had just moved to the back of the bus. He worried how this would affect his reputation and integrity. But Jack also knew he had done the right thing.

Jack remembered what his mother taught him. He was ready for this.

On August 2, 1944, the case of *The United States v. 2nd Lieutenant Jack R. Robinson* began. The prosecution witnesses described a defiant soldier who ignored a direct order and was disrespectful to a senior officer.

Jack had no choice but to listen while people lied about him. But when he took the stand, he told the truth with dignity. He described how the bus driver had ordered him to the back of the bus. How soldiers ranked beneath him treated him like a criminal instead of an officer. He testified that the MP captain never gave him any orders. That he hadn't done anything wrong.

Then Jack waited for the real story to come out.

And soon, the truth *did* emerge. Several of Jack's commanding officers testified about his excellent character and leadership skills. Some prosecution witnesses admitted that Jack had never ignored any orders because he was never given any orders. Others revealed that Jack had been called names and insulted because of his race.

After five hours of testimony, it was clear to the court that Jack had been charged only because of the color of his skin. The verdict was delivered: *Not guilty*.

Jack had fought for what he knew was right. He had stood up to prejudice and discrimination and exercised his right to sit wherever he wanted on a bus. He was one of the first black Americans to challenge a segregation law in court. And he won.

Jack made history that day.

But it wasn't the last time Jack would do that.

After the trial, Jack asked to leave the army. He took a
job in Kansas City,

and then another in Montreal.

And in 1947, Jack went to work in Brooklyn, New York. But at all those jobs, most people didn't call him Jack anymore. They called him Jackie.

Jackie Robinson.

That job he took in Kansas City was to play baseball for a Negro League team called the Monarchs. The job in Montreal was to play for a minor league team called the Royals.

And that job in Brooklyn was to play first base for the Brooklyn Dodgers.

On April 15, 1947, Jack broke the color line in professional baseball. Once again, he had to fight for what was right with patience and grace in the face of racism and hatred. And, once again, he made history.

By then, Jack had had plenty of practice doing both those things.

Timeline

May 18, 1896   The Supreme Court rules in *Plessy v. Ferguson* that state laws requiring racial segregation in public facilities under the doctrine of "separate but equal" are constitutional. This is the basis for Jim Crow laws throughout the country.

January 31, 1919   Jack Roosevelt Robinson is born in Cairo, Ga.

1920   Mallie Robinson moves her children to Pasadena, Calif.

1935   Jack graduates from Dakota Junior High School and enrolls in John Muir High School.

1936   Jack becomes the junior boys' singles champion at the Pacific Coast Negro Tennis Tournament and plays on the Pomona baseball tournament all-star team (a team that includes future Baseball Hall of Famers Ted Williams and Bob Lemon).

1937   Jack enrolls at Pasadena Junior College.

1938   On the same day, Jack sets the record for the broad jump at the National Junior College Track Championships in Pomona and then races to Glendale to help his team win the Southern California Junior College Baseball Championships (he has two hits and a stolen base).

September 1, 1939   Jack begins at UCLA. He becomes the first four-sport letterman in UCLA history—football (1939 and 1940), basketball (1940 and 1941), track and field (1940), and baseball (1940).

1941   Jack leaves UCLA.

September 1, 1941   Jack starts playing semipro football for the Honolulu Bears.

December 5, 1941   Jack leaves Honolulu to go home to California.

December 7, 1941   Pearl Harbor Naval Base is attacked by Japan.

March 18, 1942   Jack and Nate Moreland, another black player, try out for the Chicago White Sox.

April 3, 1942   Jack joins the army.

1943   Jack is promoted to second lieutenant.

March 10, 1943   The War Department issues a directive forbidding segregation on military posts or transport.

April 1, 1944   Jack becomes a platoon leader in the army.

July 6, 1944   Jack refuses to move to the back of a military bus at Fort Hood, Tex., and is arrested.

August 2, 1944   The court-martial of Jack Robinson begins. Jack is found not guilty.

November 28, 1944   Jack is honorably discharged from the army.

March 20, 1945   Jack joins the Kansas City Monarchs.

April 16, 1945   Jack, Sam Jethroe, and Marvin Williams go to a Boston Red Sox tryout at Fenway Park. Neither the manager nor the team shows up for the event.

August 28, 1945   Jack meets with Branch Rickey and joins the Dodger organization.

October 23, 1945 Jack signs a contract with the Montreal Royals.

February 10, 1946 Jack marries his college sweetheart, Rachel Isum.

April 18, 1946 Jack plays his first professional game for the Royals at Roosevelt Stadium in Jersey City, N.J.

1946 The Royals win the International League by 19½ games and win the Little World Series. Jack is the league batting champion with a .349 average in 124 games.

April 15, 1947 Jack makes his Major League Baseball debut with the Brooklyn Dodgers against the Boston Braves at Ebbets Field, Brooklyn.

July 5, 1947 The Cleveland Indians announce the signing of outfielder Larry Doby of the Newark Eagles, the second African American professional baseball player.

October 1947 Jack is voted the first ever Major League Rookie of the Year.

July 26, 1948 President Truman signs Executive Order 9981, desegregating the military.

October 10, 1948 Satchel Paige becomes the first African American player to pitch in the World Series.

October 1949 Jack is named the National League Most Valuable Player.

October 4, 1955 Jack wins his only championship when the Brooklyn Dodgers beat the New York Yankees in seven games.

December 1, 1955 Rosa Parks, a civil rights activist and the secretary of the Montgomery, Ala., chapter of the NAACP, refuses to give up her seat to a white passenger in violation of the segregation law. She is arrested. Parks is convicted of disorderly conduct and violating a local ordinance and fined $10, plus $4 in court costs.

December 5, 1955 The black community of Montgomery launches a bus boycott that eventually lasts for 381 days.

December 17, 1956 The Supreme Court rules in *Browder v. Gayle* that bus segregation is unconstitutional under the Fourteenth Amendment.

December 20, 1956 Alabama is ordered to desegregate buses.

January 5, 1957 Jack retires from baseball.

July 21, 1959 The Boston Red Sox become the last team in Major League Baseball to integrate.

July 23, 1962 Jack is inducted into the Baseball Hall of Fame.

August 28, 1963 Martin Luther King Jr. gives his "I Have a Dream" speech from the steps of the Lincoln Memorial during the March on Washington.

July 2, 1964 Congress enacts the Civil Rights Act of 1964, outlawing discrimination based on race, color, religion, sex, or national origin.

August 6, 1965 President Johnson signs the Voting Rights Act of 1965 into law.

October 24, 1972 Jack R. Robinson passes away.

April 15, 1997 Major League Baseball retires the number 42 in honor of Jack.

Author Note

These days, Americans consider Jackie Robinson to be a national hero, an American icon. It is hard for many of us who have grown up after segregation, after school integration, after the bus boycotts and sit-ins and marches, and after the Civil Rights Act and the Voting Rights Act of 1965, to imagine that things could be different— and how different they truly were. But the America that Jackie Robinson grew up in would probably be as unrecognizable a landscape to most of us today as the surface of the moon.

These are the kinds of signs that Jackie Robinson and scores of other Americans of color faced every day:

WE WANT WHITE TENANTS IN OUR WHITE COMMUNITY

NO DOGS, NEGROES, MEXICANS

WAITING ROOM FOR COLORED ONLY, BY ORDER POLICE DEPT

THIS PART OF THE BUS FOR COLORED RACE

PUBLIC SWIMMING POOL, WHITE ONLY

Today, most of us can't imagine being faced with signs like these, or even hearing language like this. But in the early part of the twentieth century, these kinds of attitudes were considered acceptable, just as it was acceptable to call an African American a "colored person" or a "Negro." It actually wasn't until the 1970s that the term "African American" became widely used.

It took the courage of people like Jackie Robinson, who were willing to stand up to the racism that was entrenched and rooted deep in American culture, to change our country and to change the way people thought about each other. Because even though these attitudes were considered acceptable by some white people back in those days, we all know now that they really weren't acceptable at all.

Jackie was just one of many, many people who fought hard to eliminate legal segregation in the United States. But the fight did not end in the 1960s and 1970s. There are still so many walls to tear down and bridges to build. Jackie once said, "I believe in the goodness of a free society. And I believe that society can remain good only as long as we are willing to fight for it—and to fight against whatever imperfections may exist." It's important to remember that every big change in the world starts with someone making a choice—like staying in his seat on the bus or showing up to play baseball with hostile players and in front of angry crowds—that might seem small in the moment. But even the smallest choices can have huge consequences; even the smallest moments can change the world forever.

Bibliography

Falkner, David. *Great Time Coming: The Life of Jackie Robinson, from Baseball to Birmingham.* New York: Simon & Schuster, 1996.

Rampersad, Arnold. *Jackie Robinson: A Biography.* New York: Ballantine, 1998.

Robinson, Jackie, and Alfred Duckett. *I Never Had It Made: An Autobiography of Jackie Robinson.* New York: Ecco, 2003.

Tygiel, Jules. *Baseball's Great Experiment: Jackie Robinson and His Legacy.* Oxford: Oxford University Press, 1983

Tygiel, Jules. *"The Court-Martial of Jackie Robinson." American Heritage Magazine* 35:5 (August–September 1984), www.americanheritage.com/content/court-martial-jackie-robinson.

Vernon, John. *"Jim Crow, Meet Lieutenant Robinson: A 1944 Court-Martial." Prologue Magazine* 40:1 (Spring 2008), www.archives.gov/publications/prologue/2008/spring/robinson.html.